DATE DUE			OCT 04
AUG 22 06			
JAN 1 7 '07			
GAYLORD			PRINTED IN U.S.A.

A Pet's Life

Hamsters

Anita Ganeri

Heinemann Library
Chicago, Illinois

Design by Richard Parker and Tinstar Design Limited (www.tinstar.co.uk)
Originated by Dot Gradations
Printed and bound in China by South China Printing Company

07 06 05 04
10 9 8 7 6 5 4 3 2

Library of Congress Cataloging-in-Publication Data
Ganeri, Anita, 1961-
     Hamsters / Anita Ganeri.
          v. cm. -- (A pet's life) (Heinemann first library)
Includes bibliographical references and index.
Contents: What is a hamster? -- Hamster babies -- Your pet hamster -- Choosing your hamster -- Preparing your cage -- Welcome home -- Hamster play-time -- Feeding time -- Cleaning the cage -- Growing up -- A healthy hamster -- Old age.
     ISBN 1-4034-3997-4 (hardback) -- ISBN 1-4034-4273-8 (pbk.) 1. Hamsters as pets--Juvenile literature. [1. Hamsters. 2. Pets.] I. Title. II. Series.
     SF459.H3G34 2003
     636.9'356--dc21
                                                     2002151590

Acknowledgments
The author and publishers are grateful to the followir for permission to reproduce copyright material: pp. 4, 5 Dorling Kindersley Images; p. 6 Ardea /I. R. Beames; p. 7 Alamy Images; p. 8 Oxford Scientific Films/Renee Stockdale/AA; pp. 9, 13, 14, 17, 18, 19, 20, 21, 22, 23 Haddon Davies; pp. 10, 11, 15, 16 Tudor Photography; p. 12 Armitage Pet Care.

Cover photograph of hamster reproduced with permission of Getty Images/G. K. & Vikki Hart.

The publishers would like to thank Jacque Schultz, CPDT, Lila Miller, DVM, and Stephen Zawistowski, Ph.D., CAAB of the ASPCA™ for their assistance in the preparation of this book.

Also, special thanks to expert reader, Dr. Roberta Drell, Morton Grove Animal Hospital, Morton Grove, Illinois.

Every effort has been made to contact copyright holders of any material reproduced in this book. Any omissions will be rectified in subsequent printings if notice is given to the publisher.

ASPCA™ and The American Society for the Prevention of Cruelty to Animals™ are registered trademarks of The American Society for the Prevention of Cruelty to Animals.

Some words are shown in bold, **like this.** You can find out what they mean by looking in the glossary.

Contents

What Is a Hamster?

Hamsters make good pets. The most popular kind of hamster is the golden Syrian hamster. It gets its name from the color of its fur.

There are many different kinds of hamsters.

Here you can see the different parts of a hamster's body and what each part does.

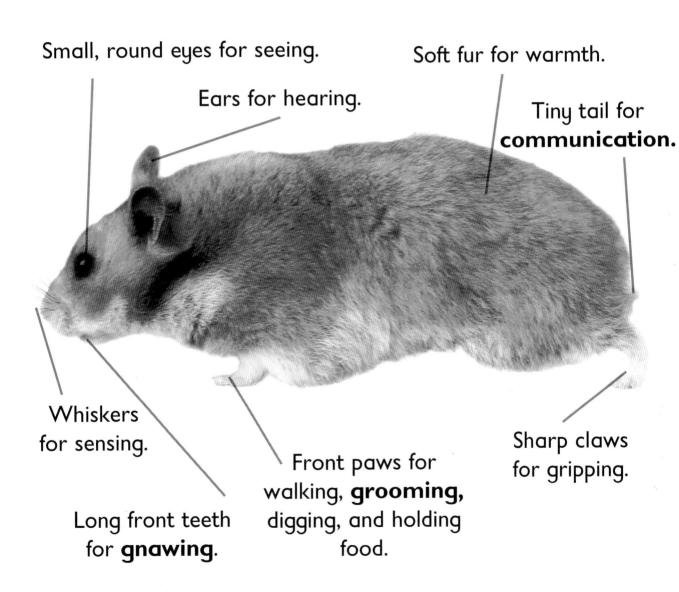

Small, round eyes for seeing.

Ears for hearing.

Soft fur for warmth.

Tiny tail for **communication.**

Whiskers for sensing.

Front paws for walking, **grooming,** digging, and holding food.

Long front teeth for **gnawing**.

Sharp claws for gripping.

Hamster Babies

Baby hamsters are called **cubs.** They are born with no fur and with their eyes closed. A mother hamster has about five to nine cubs in a **litter.**

The mother hamster feeds milk to her cubs.

The cubs are old enough to leave their mother when they are about four weeks old. They are then ready to become pets.

At three weeks old, the cubs start to play.

Your Pet Hamster

Hamsters are fun to keep as pets.
They can be quite easy to take care of,
but you must care for your hamster
properly.

You need time
to feed your
hamster and
play with it
every day.

If you go away on vacation, make sure that someone looks after your hamster. Ask a friend or neighbor to come over every day.

Your hamster must always have food, fresh water, and clean bedding.

Choosing Your Hamster

You can buy a hamster from a pet store or from a hamster **breeder.** You can also adopt a hamster from an **animal shelter.**

Pick a lively hamster. A shy or nervous-looking hamster may not be healthy.

Choose a chubby hamster with soft, shiny fur. Be sure that its skin is free of sores or bald spots. Check that its bottom is dry and clean.

A healthy hamster's eyes, ears, teeth, mouth, and nose should be clean.

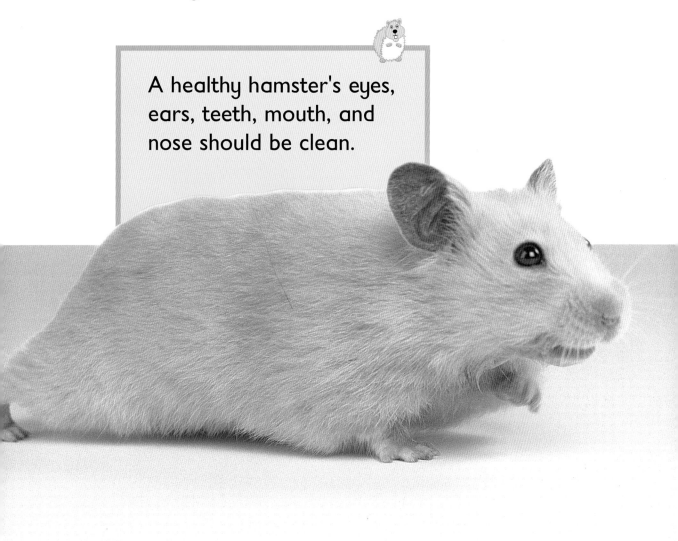

Preparing the Cage

Hamsters are very lively. They like to run and climb. Your hamster needs a large cage in which to live and a **nest box** for sleeping.

A set of round, stacking cages connect to make a good home.

Put a layer of unscented hardwood **shavings** on the floor of the cage. Fill the nest box with shredded paper for bedding. Do not use newspaper.

Put the cage in a warm place that is out of bright sunlight.

Welcome Home

You can bring your hamster home in a small cardboard box. Make sure that the box has holes in it so that your hamster gets some air.

At home, put your hamster in its cage. Leave it alone for a few hours to get used to its new home.

Be gentle when you pick up your hamster. Move slowly and quietly. Otherwise your hamster may get scared and try to bite you.

To pick up your hamster, scoop it up gently with both hands.

Play Time

Hamsters need lots of exercise. Put an exercise wheel in the cage. The wheel should not have holes in it. That way, your hamster will not trap its feet.

Jars, cardboard tubes, and climbing frames also make good toys.

If you let your pet out of its cage, shut all the doors and windows. Hamsters can run very fast. They are small and hard to find.

Let your hamster climb from one of your hands to the other.

Feeding Time

Hamsters like to eat seeds, nuts, and grains. You can buy them mixed from a pet store. You can also feed your hamster some fresh fruit and vegetables.

Hamsters like to store food in **pouches** in their cheeks. They eat the food later.

You should feed your hamster once a day, in the evening. Put the food in a heavy dish so that it does not tip over.

Make sure that your pet always has fresh water to drink. Attach a water bottle to the cage.

Cleaning the Cage

You can help your hamster stay healthy by keeping its cage clean. Every day, remove any **droppings** and pieces of leftover food.

Wash out the food bowl and water bottle every day.

Every week, give the whole cage a complete cleaning. Change the layer of unscented hardwood **shavings** on the floor. Put some fresh bedding in the **nest box.**

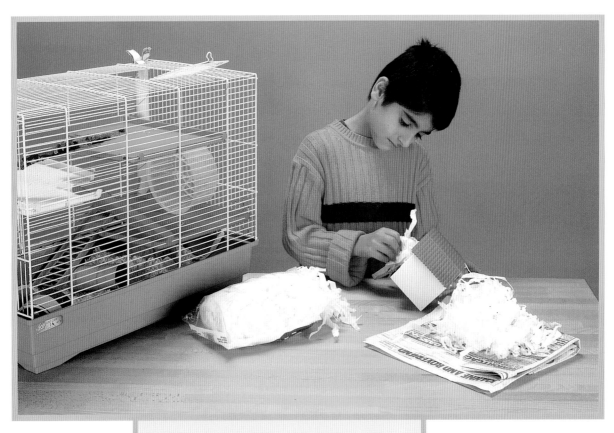

Always wash your hands after cleaning your hamster's cage.

Growing Up

Hamsters grow very quickly. An adult Syrian hamster is about 4 inches (10 centimeters) long and weighs about 3.5 ounces (100 grams).

A hamster can easily fit in your hands.

Golden Syrian hamsters like to live on their own. If you put two of them in the same cage, they may fight with each other. Never keep a hamster in a cage with other animals.

Female Russian hamsters can live together if they have been together all their lives.

A Healthy Hamster

Your hamster will stay healthy if you care for it properly. But hamsters can catch colds and the flu from people. A wet tail is another sign of sickness.

You should take your hamster to the **veterinarian** if it looks sick.

Your hamster's front teeth grow all the time. If its teeth grow too long, your hamster may not be able to eat properly.

Give your hamster a wooden **gnawing** block to wear its teeth down.

25

Old Age

If you look after your hamster, it may live for about two to three years. As it gets older, it might lose some fur and gain weight.

An old hamster might need special care.

Older hamsters still need to be cared for every day. You should still feed them, play with them, and clean their cages.

Caring for your hamster will help you learn how to treat animals properly.

Useful Tips

- Hamsters wake up at night. Put the cage in a place where it will not bother you.

- Do not wake your hamster up during the day to play. It might bite you.

- Keep the cage out of reach of cats and other pets.

- Hamsters clean their fur with their front paws. But you need to brush long-haired hamsters gently every day with a soft toothbrush.

- Let your hamster sniff your fingers. It will get to know you by how you smell.

Fact File

- Wild hamsters live in the desert.

- Wild hamsters spend the day sleeping in **burrows** under the ground. This keeps them cool.

- All pet golden hamsters come from one family found in the desert in Syria in 1930.

- The name *hamster* comes from a German word which means hoarder. This is because hamsters **hoard** food in their cheeks.

- An adult hamster needs about 1/2 ounce (15 grams) of food a day. That's about a teaspoonful.

- Hamsters are nearsighted. They cannot see very well.

Glossary

animal shelter place where lost or unwanted animals are looked after and found new homes
breeder someone who raises animals
burrow hole or tunnel in the ground
communication how animals talk to each other and to you
cub baby hamster
dropping waste from the body
gnaw chew and bite
groom gently brush and clean your hamster's fur. Hamsters also groom themselves.
hoard store or keep for later
litter group of hamster babies
nest box box filled with bedding in which your hamster sleeps
pouches spaces in a hamster's cheeks where it stores food
shaving thin slice or strip of wood
veterinarian doctor who cares for animals

More Books to Read

An older reader can help you with these books.

Bartlett, Patricia Pope. *The Hamster Handbook.* Hauppauge, N.Y.: Barron's Educational Publishing, 2003.

Carroll, David. *The ASPCA Complete Guide to Pet Care.* New York: Dutton/Plume, 2001.

Foran, Jill. *Caring for Your Hamster.* Mankato, Minn.: Weigl Publishers, Incorporated, 2003.

Nelson, Robin. *Pet Hamster.* Minneapolis, Minn.: Lerner Publishing Group, 2002.

Thomas, Lyn. *My Pet Hamster.* Tonawanda, N.Y.: Kids Can Press, Limited, 2002.

A Note from the ASPCA™

Pets are often our good friends for the very best of reasons. They don't care how we look, how we dress, or who our friends are. They like us because we are nice to them and take care of them. That's what being friends is all about.

This book has given you information to help you know what your pet needs. Learn all you can from this book and others, and from people who know about animals, such as veterinarians and workers at animal shelters like the ASPCA™. You will soon become your pet's most important friend.

Index